MY HOME ED JOURNAL

EDUCATIONAL EXPERIENCES ARE ALL AROUND US

MY HOME ED JOURNAL

BROOKE MCCLURE · LUCY SPENCER

Copyright © 2020 by Education Boutique

All rights reserved.

No part of this book may be reproduced or used in any manner without written permission of the copyright owner.

Cover Design and interior formatting: Mark Thomas / Coverness.com

ISBN 9798605103905

www.educationboutique.co.uk

Table of Contents

Preface .... *i*

How to Use This Journal .... *iii*

Personal Profile *1*

    Example of a Journal Entry *2*

    Journal Entry Pages .... *4 - 83*

    Holiday Journal Entry Pages .... *84 - 95*

Learning by Topic Frameworks Explained *97*

    Example of a Learning by Topic Framework – Sustainable Eating *98*

Glossary of Terms–Mathematics *105*

Glossary of Terms–English *109*

Preface

In 2019, the Children's Commissioner suggested the figure of registered home educated pupils in the UK was over 60,000 but could be as high as 80,000. Despite these ever-growing figures, there is a stark lack of support and guidelines for families to follow.

This journal can be used whether you are flexi-schooling, unschooling or in structured home education.

Education Boutique view home education as an exciting opportunity to create a unique learning journey. *My Home Ed Journal* will serve as a motivating and fun guide that documents your educational experiences and encourages self-reflection.

How to Use This Journal

- This journal was created for you to record your educational experiences and interests. Your journal will be as unique as your learning journey. You may visit a museum and be inspired to focus your learning around your experience for a week or maybe you will choose to focus on a broad topic like 'slime' for a month! You can choose!
- At the top of each weekly page is a reading log. Reading doesn't have to be in the form of a book; newspaper and magazine articles, audio books, comic books, instructions for a recipe or assembling an object and blogs can be just as helpful in developing your reading skills. It's a great idea to record how many minutes (or hours!) you read each day.
- We know you won't always choose to take half terms and holidays at the same time as schools, so we have grouped optional holiday pages in the journal. During any holidays we would encourage you to collect and stick in any photographs and/or mementoes (e.g. train tickets, leaflets etc.) from your experiences.
- At the back of the journal you will find two useful sections. The first is a space to record any online learning resources you come across that you consider particularly useful and that you want to remember for future reference. The second is a glossary of maths and English terms.

For your parents/guardians/teachers:

It is important to point out your key role as a home educating facilitator is to link what you have done during a week to these core subjects: English, maths and science. On pages 97-99 you will find examples of how to make these links. Our *Learning by Topic Framework* shows you how your child's interests can be turned into a topic of study for an entire term. We should all encourage hands on and interactive learning that promotes thinking outside the box - maths does not have to mean sitting down and completing a worksheet of sums.

Keeping this journal up to date will help you feel in control and also save you time in collating evidence for Local Authorities (LA) should they contact you.

Name: _____

All about me!

Age: _____

PERSONAL PROFILE

Birthday / star sign

Photo or drawing of me!

Close Family or Friends:
_____
_____
_____
_____

Pets: _____

Favourite Topic to learn about: _____

Some of my favourite things (e.g. book, TV show, app, game, music):
_____

Favourite inspirational quote / meme:
_____

Strengths (what I'm good at):
_____

Areas I would like to improve:
_____
_____

Date: 1st September 2020

READING

Use this log to record what you read and the amount of time you spend reading each

Monday	Tuesday	Wednesday	Thursday	Friday	Weekend
First News (Newspaper for kids)	Reading/making a cake mixture. Audio book: War Horse	Audio book: War Horse First News	Audio book: War Horse The Avengers (comic book)	Visited the Science Museum, read leaflets.	The Cadwaladr Quests: Tangled Time
20mins	20mins / 30mins	15mins / 30mins	15mins / 30mins	1 hour	2 hours

EDUCATIONAL EXPERIENCES

Use the spaces below to record the educational experiences you complete this week.

ENGLISH EXPERIENCES:

- I carried out research on sustainable eating and followed up with a three paragraph summary.
- Created a crossword puzzle using my theme words (my theme words are from my topic of study: sustainable eating).
- I wrote a letter to members of my local community encouraging them to shop locally and eat seasonally. I then made a recording of this in the style of a vlog.
- I have started to draft a poem about sustainable eating (in sonnet format).

MATHEMATICS EXPERIENCES:

- Looked up the figures of deforestation rates over the past decade and plotted this information on a line graph.
- Measured the perimeter and area of my garden and planter boxes.
- I took photographs of angles that I found in my garden. Then on my computer, I sorted the images into a table under the following headings: acute angles, right angles, obtuse angles, straight angles and reflex angles.
- Created some number codes using my theme words and my father was able to crack 9 out of 10 of them!

SCIENCE EXPERIENCES:

- Have started to research which plants will grow in my garden during the four seasons. Over the coming weeks I will plant some seeds and I want to plan it so I can grow fresh produce in my garden all year round.
- I visited the Science Museum with my mother and enjoyed the codebreaking exhibition. From what I discovered and with a little more research I constructed a timeline of the history of coding.

EDUCATIONAL OUTINGS

- My local library
- Science Museum
- Visited my Grandparents and discussed impacts to the environment over time.

Quote of the Week

'You don't have to be great to start, but you have to start to be great.'

— Zig Ziglar

OTHER EDUCATIONAL EXPERIENCES

Use this space to record educational experiences you complete this week in other learning areas

e.g. art, music, wellness and wellbeing, computer skills, history, sports, environmental studies, languages, building and construction.

- Yoga and meditating, football and swimming
- Coding club at my local library
- Piano Practice
- Language learning app (Dulingo) – French
- Sketching tutorials (YouTube)
- Recycling project – an ongoing project
- History of coding
- Building a bird feeder – an ongoing project

THE BEST PART OF MY WEEK:

I really enjoyed writing my letter to convince people to shop locally and eat seasonally. It was fun to then film myself and turn it into a vlog! I showed it to my next-door neighbour and she said it had inspired her to try and shop locally when possible and that she would put a lot more thought into cooking and eating by season!

QUESTIONS I WOULD LIKE TO EXPLORE FURTHER:

Which plants grow best during different seasons?
I need to carry out further research on what grows best in cooler conditions.

MY GOALS FOR NEXT WEEK:

- Finish my poem.
- Finish researching plants.
- Carry on with my recycling project.
- Carry on with building my bird feeder.

Date: _____

READING

Use this log to record what you read and the amount of time you spend reading each

Monday	Tuesday	Wednesday	Thursday	Friday	Weekend

EDUCATIONAL EXPERIENCES

Use the spaces below to record the educational experiences you complete this week.

ENGLISH EXPERIENCES:

MATHEMATICS EXPERIENCES:

SCIENCE EXPERIENCES:

EDUCATIONAL OUTINGS

Quote of the Week

'You don't have to be great to start, but you have to start to be great.'

— Zig Ziglar

OTHER EDUCATIONAL EXPERIENCES

Use this space to record educational experiences you complete this week in other learning areas

e.g. art, music, wellness and wellbeing, computer skills, history, sports, environmental studies, languages, building and construction.

THE BEST PART OF MY WEEK:

QUESTIONS I WOULD LIKE TO EXPLORE FURTHER:

MY GOALS FOR NEXT WEEK:

Date: _____

READING

Use this log to record what you read and the amount of time you spend reading each

| *Monday* | *Tuesday* | *Wednesday* | *Thursday* | *Friday* | *Weekend* |

EDUCATIONAL EXPERIENCES

Use the spaces below to record the educational experiences you complete this week.

ENGLISH EXPERIENCES:

MATHEMATICS EXPERIENCES:

SCIENCE EXPERIENCES:

EDUCATIONAL OUTINGS

Quote of the Week

'The beautiful thing about learning is nobody can take it away from you.'

— B.B. King

OTHER EDUCATIONAL EXPERIENCES

Use this space to record educational experiences you complete this week in other learning areas

e.g. art, music, wellness and wellbeing, computer skills, history, sports, environmental studies, languages, building and construction.

THE BEST PART OF MY WEEK:

QUESTIONS I WOULD LIKE TO EXPLORE FURTHER:

MY GOALS FOR NEXT WEEK:

Date: _____

READING

Use this log to record what you read and the amount of time you spend reading each

Monday	*Tuesday*	*Wednesday*	*Thursday*	*Friday*	*Weekend*

EDUCATIONAL EXPERIENCES

Use the spaces below to record the educational experiences you complete this week.

ENGLISH EXPERIENCES:

MATHEMATICS EXPERIENCES:

SCIENCE EXPERIENCES:

EDUCATIONAL OUTINGS

Quote of the Week

'Optimism is the faith that leads to achievement.'

— Helen Keller

OTHER EDUCATIONAL EXPERIENCES

Use this space to record educational experiences you complete this week in other learning areas

e.g. art, music, wellness and wellbeing, computer skills, history, sports, environmental studies, languages, building and construction.

THE BEST PART OF MY WEEK:

QUESTIONS I WOULD LIKE TO EXPLORE FURTHER:

MY GOALS FOR NEXT WEEK:

Date: _____

READING

Use this log to record what you read and the amount of time you spend reading each

Monday	*Tuesday*	*Wednesday*	*Thursday*	*Friday*	*Weekend*

EDUCATIONAL EXPERIENCES

Use the spaces below to record the educational experiences you complete this week.

ENGLISH EXPERIENCES:

MATHEMATICS EXPERIENCES:

SCIENCE EXPERIENCES:

EDUCATIONAL OUTINGS

Quote of the Week

'Nothing is impossible. The word itself says I'M POSSIBLE!'

— Audrey Hepburn

OTHER EDUCATIONAL EXPERIENCES

Use this space to record educational experiences you complete this week in other learning areas

e.g. art, music, wellness and wellbeing, computer skills, history, sports, environmental studies, languages, building and construction.

THE BEST PART OF MY WEEK:

QUESTIONS I WOULD LIKE TO EXPLORE FURTHER:

MY GOALS FOR NEXT WEEK:

Date: _____

READING

Use this log to record what you read and the amount of time you spend reading each

Monday	*Tuesday*	*Wednesday*	*Thursday*	*Friday*	*Weekend*

EDUCATIONAL EXPERIENCES

Use the spaces below to record the educational experiences you complete this week.

ENGLISH EXPERIENCES:

MATHEMATICS EXPERIENCES:

SCIENCE EXPERIENCES:

EDUCATIONAL OUTINGS

Quote of the Week

'Never let formal education get in the way of your learning.'

— Mark Twain

OTHER EDUCATIONAL EXPERIENCES

Use this space to record educational experiences you complete this week in other learning areas

e.g. art, music, wellness and wellbeing, computer skills, history, sports, environmental studies, languages, building and construction.

THE BEST PART OF MY WEEK:

QUESTIONS I WOULD LIKE TO EXPLORE FURTHER:

MY GOALS FOR NEXT WEEK:

Date: _____

READING

Use this log to record what you read and the amount of time you spend reading each

Monday	Tuesday	Wednesday	Thursday	Friday	Weekend

EDUCATIONAL EXPERIENCES

Use the spaces below to record the educational experiences you complete this week.

ENGLISH EXPERIENCES:

MATHEMATICS EXPERIENCES:

SCIENCE EXPERIENCES:

EDUCATIONAL OUTINGS

Quote of the Week

'Think left and think right and think low and think high. Oh, the thinks you can think up if only you try!'
— Theodor Seuss Geisel

OTHER EDUCATIONAL EXPERIENCES

Use this space to record educational experiences you complete this week in other learning areas

e.g. art, music, wellness and wellbeing, computer skills, history, sports, environmental studies, languages, building and construction.

THE BEST PART OF MY WEEK:

QUESTIONS I WOULD LIKE TO EXPLORE FURTHER:

MY GOALS FOR NEXT WEEK:

Date: _____

READING

Use this log to record what you read and the amount of time you spend reading each

Monday	*Tuesday*	*Wednesday*	*Thursday*	*Friday*	*Weekend*

EDUCATIONAL EXPERIENCES

Use the spaces below to record the educational experiences you complete this week.

ENGLISH EXPERIENCES:

MATHEMATICS EXPERIENCES:

SCIENCE EXPERIENCES:

EDUCATIONAL OUTINGS

Quote of the Week

'In order to be irreplaceable one must always be different.'

— Coco Chanel

OTHER EDUCATIONAL EXPERIENCES

Use this space to record educational experiences you complete this week in other learning areas

e.g. art, music, wellness and wellbeing, computer skills, history, sports, environmental studies, languages, building and construction.

THE BEST PART OF MY WEEK:

QUESTIONS I WOULD LIKE TO EXPLORE FURTHER:

MY GOALS FOR NEXT WEEK:

Date: _____

READING

Use this log to record what you read and the amount of time you spend reading each

Monday	*Tuesday*	*Wednesday*	*Thursday*	*Friday*	*Weekend*

EDUCATIONAL EXPERIENCES

Use the spaces below to record the educational experiences you complete this week.

ENGLISH EXPERIENCES:

MATHEMATICS EXPERIENCES:

SCIENCE EXPERIENCES:

EDUCATIONAL OUTINGS

Quote of the Week

'You must do the things you think you cannot do.'
— Eleanor Roosevelt

OTHER EDUCATIONAL EXPERIENCES

Use this space to record educational experiences you complete this week in other learning areas

e.g. art, music, wellness and wellbeing, computer skills, history, sports, environmental studies, languages, building and construction.

THE BEST PART OF MY WEEK:

QUESTIONS I WOULD LIKE TO EXPLORE FURTHER:

MY GOALS FOR NEXT WEEK:

Date: _____

READING

Use this log to record what you read and the amount of time you spend reading each

Monday	*Tuesday*	*Wednesday*	*Thursday*	*Friday*	*Weekend*

EDUCATIONAL EXPERIENCES

Use the spaces below to record the educational experiences you complete this week.

ENGLISH EXPERIENCES:

MATHEMATICS EXPERIENCES:

SCIENCE EXPERIENCES:

EDUCATIONAL OUTINGS

Quote of the Week

'The purpose of learning is growth, and our minds, unlike our bodies, can continue growing as we continue to live.'
— Mortimer Adler

OTHER EDUCATIONAL EXPERIENCES

Use this space to record educational experiences you complete this week in other learning areas

e.g. art, music, wellness and wellbeing, computer skills, history, sports, environmental studies, languages, building and construction.

THE BEST PART OF MY WEEK:

QUESTIONS I WOULD LIKE TO EXPLORE FURTHER:

MY GOALS FOR NEXT WEEK:

Date: _____

READING

Use this log to record what you read and the amount of time you spend reading each

Monday	*Tuesday*	*Wednesday*	*Thursday*	*Friday*	*Weekend*

EDUCATIONAL EXPERIENCES

Use the spaces below to record the educational experiences you complete this week.

ENGLISH EXPERIENCES:

MATHEMATICS EXPERIENCES:

SCIENCE EXPERIENCES:

EDUCATIONAL OUTINGS

Quote of the Week

'You don't learn to walk by following rules. You learn by doing, and by falling over.

— Richard Branson

OTHER EDUCATIONAL EXPERIENCES

Use this space to record educational experiences you complete this week in other learning areas

e.g. art, music, wellness and wellbeing, computer skills, history, sports, environmental studies, languages, building and construction.

THE BEST PART OF MY WEEK:

QUESTIONS I WOULD LIKE TO EXPLORE FURTHER:

MY GOALS FOR NEXT WEEK:

Date: _____

READING

Use this log to record what you read and the amount of time you spend reading each

Monday	*Tuesday*	*Wednesday*	*Thursday*	*Friday*	*Weekend*

EDUCATIONAL EXPERIENCES

Use the spaces below to record the educational experiences you complete this week.

ENGLISH EXPERIENCES:

MATHEMATICS EXPERIENCES:

SCIENCE EXPERIENCES:

EDUCATIONAL OUTINGS

Quote of the Week

'Education is one thing no one can take away from you.'

— Elin Nordegren

OTHER EDUCATIONAL EXPERIENCES

Use this space to record educational experiences you complete this week in other learning areas

e.g. art, music, wellness and wellbeing, computer skills, history, sports, environmental studies, languages, building and construction.

THE BEST PART OF MY WEEK:

QUESTIONS I WOULD LIKE TO EXPLORE FURTHER:

MY GOALS FOR NEXT WEEK:

Date: _____

READING

Use this log to record what you read and the amount of time you spend reading each

Monday	*Tuesday*	*Wednesday*	*Thursday*	*Friday*	*Weekend*

EDUCATIONAL EXPERIENCES

Use the spaces below to record the educational experiences you complete this week.

ENGLISH EXPERIENCES:

MATHEMATICS EXPERIENCES:

SCIENCE EXPERIENCES:

EDUCATIONAL OUTINGS

Quote of the Week

'The more you read, the more things you will know. The more that you learn, the more places you'll go.'
— Theodor Seuss Geisel

OTHER EDUCATIONAL EXPERIENCES

Use this space to record educational experiences you complete this week in other learning areas

e.g. art, music, wellness and wellbeing, computer skills, history, sports, environmental studies, languages, building and construction.

THE BEST PART OF MY WEEK:

QUESTIONS I WOULD LIKE TO EXPLORE FURTHER:

MY GOALS FOR NEXT WEEK:

Date: _____

READING

Use this log to record what you read and the amount of time you spend reading each

Monday	Tuesday	Wednesday	Thursday	Friday	Weekend

EDUCATIONAL EXPERIENCES

Use the spaces below to record the educational experiences you complete this week.

ENGLISH EXPERIENCES:

MATHEMATICS EXPERIENCES:

SCIENCE EXPERIENCES:

EDUCATIONAL OUTINGS

Quote of the Week

'Tell me and I forget, teach me and I may remember, involve me and I learn.'
— Benjamin Franklin

OTHER EDUCATIONAL EXPERIENCES

Use this space to record educational experiences you complete this week in other learning areas

e.g. art, music, wellness and wellbeing, computer skills, history, sports, environmental studies, languages, building and construction.

THE BEST PART OF MY WEEK:

QUESTIONS I WOULD LIKE TO EXPLORE FURTHER:

MY GOALS FOR NEXT WEEK:

Date: _____

READING

Use this log to record what you read and the amount of time you spend reading each

Monday	*Tuesday*	*Wednesday*	*Thursday*	*Friday*	*Weekend*

EDUCATIONAL EXPERIENCES

Use the spaces below to record the educational experiences you complete this week.

ENGLISH EXPERIENCES:

MATHEMATICS EXPERIENCES:

SCIENCE EXPERIENCES:

EDUCATIONAL OUTINGS

Quote of the Week

'It's not about how much you do, but how much love you put into what you do that counts.'
— Mother Teresa

OTHER EDUCATIONAL EXPERIENCES

Use this space to record educational experiences you complete this week in other learning areas

e.g. art, music, wellness and wellbeing, computer skills, history, sports, environmental studies, languages, building and construction.

THE BEST PART OF MY WEEK:

QUESTIONS I WOULD LIKE TO EXPLORE FURTHER:

MY GOALS FOR NEXT WEEK:

Date: _____

READING

Use this log to record what you read and the amount of time you spend reading each

Monday	Tuesday	Wednesday	Thursday	Friday	Weekend

EDUCATIONAL EXPERIENCES

Use the spaces below to record the educational experiences you complete this week.

ENGLISH EXPERIENCES:

MATHEMATICS EXPERIENCES:

SCIENCE EXPERIENCES:

EDUCATIONAL OUTINGS

Quote of the Week

'We do not need magic to change the world, we carry all the power we need inside ourselves already: we have the power to imagine better.'

— J.K. Rowling

OTHER EDUCATIONAL EXPERIENCES

Use this space to record educational experiences you complete this week in other learning areas

e.g. art, music, wellness and wellbeing, computer skills, history, sports, environmental studies, languages, building and construction.

THE BEST PART OF MY WEEK:

QUESTIONS I WOULD LIKE TO EXPLORE FURTHER:

MY GOALS FOR NEXT WEEK:

Date: _____

READING

Use this log to record what you read and the amount of time you spend reading each

Monday	Tuesday	Wednesday	Thursday	Friday	Weekend

EDUCATIONAL EXPERIENCES

Use the spaces below to record the educational experiences you complete this week.

ENGLISH EXPERIENCES:

MATHEMATICS EXPERIENCES:

SCIENCE EXPERIENCES:

EDUCATIONAL OUTINGS

Quote of the Week

'Anyone who stops learning is old, whether at eighty or twenty. Anyone who keeps learning stays young.'

— Henry Ford

OTHER EDUCATIONAL EXPERIENCES

Use this space to record educational experiences you complete this week in other learning areas

e.g. art, music, wellness and wellbeing, computer skills, history, sports, environmental studies, languages, building and construction.

THE BEST PART OF MY WEEK:

QUESTIONS I WOULD LIKE TO EXPLORE FURTHER:

MY GOALS FOR NEXT WEEK:

Date: _____

READING

Use this log to record what you read and the amount of time you spend reading each

Monday	*Tuesday*	*Wednesday*	*Thursday*	*Friday*	*Weekend*

EDUCATIONAL EXPERIENCES

Use the spaces below to record the educational experiences you complete this week.

ENGLISH EXPERIENCES:

MATHEMATICS EXPERIENCES:

SCIENCE EXPERIENCES:

EDUCATIONAL OUTINGS

Quote of the Week

'Most of the important things in the world have been accomplished by people who have kept on trying when there seemed to be no hope at all.'
— Dale Carnegie

OTHER EDUCATIONAL EXPERIENCES

Use this space to record educational experiences you complete this week in other learning areas

e.g. art, music, wellness and wellbeing, computer skills, history, sports, environmental studies, languages, building and construction.

THE BEST PART OF MY WEEK:

QUESTIONS I WOULD LIKE TO EXPLORE FURTHER:

MY GOALS FOR NEXT WEEK:

Date: _____

READING

Use this log to record what you read and the amount of time you spend reading each

Monday	*Tuesday*	*Wednesday*	*Thursday*	*Friday*	*Weekend*

EDUCATIONAL EXPERIENCES

Use the spaces below to record the educational experiences you complete this week.

ENGLISH EXPERIENCES:

MATHEMATICS EXPERIENCES:

SCIENCE EXPERIENCES:

EDUCATIONAL OUTINGS

Quote of the Week

'I attribute my success to this — I never gave or took any excuse.'

— Florence Nightingale

OTHER EDUCATIONAL EXPERIENCES

Use this space to record educational experiences you complete this week in other learning areas

e.g. art, music, wellness and wellbeing, computer skills, history, sports, environmental studies, languages, building and construction.

THE BEST PART OF MY WEEK:

QUESTIONS I WOULD LIKE TO EXPLORE FURTHER:

MY GOALS FOR NEXT WEEK:

Date: _____

READING

Use this log to record what you read and the amount of time you spend reading each

Monday	*Tuesday*	*Wednesday*	*Thursday*	*Friday*	*Weekend*

EDUCATIONAL EXPERIENCES

Use the spaces below to record the educational experiences you complete this week.

ENGLISH EXPERIENCES:

MATHEMATICS EXPERIENCES:

SCIENCE EXPERIENCES:

EDUCATIONAL OUTINGS

Quote of the Week

'Education is not the filling of a pot but the lighting of a fire.'
— W.B. Yeats

OTHER EDUCATIONAL EXPERIENCES

Use this space to record educational experiences you complete this week in other learning areas

e.g. art, music, wellness and wellbeing, computer skills, history, sports, environmental studies, languages, building and construction.

THE BEST PART OF MY WEEK:

QUESTIONS I WOULD LIKE TO EXPLORE FURTHER:

MY GOALS FOR NEXT WEEK:

Date: _____

READING

Use this log to record what you read and the amount of time you spend reading each

Monday	Tuesday	Wednesday	Thursday	Friday	Weekend

EDUCATIONAL EXPERIENCES

Use the spaces below to record the educational experiences you complete this week.

ENGLISH EXPERIENCES:

MATHEMATICS EXPERIENCES:

SCIENCE EXPERIENCES:

EDUCATIONAL OUTINGS

Quote of the Week

'Education is the most powerful weapon which you can use to change the world.'
— Nelson Mandela

OTHER EDUCATIONAL EXPERIENCES

Use this space to record educational experiences you complete this week in other learning areas

e.g. art, music, wellness and wellbeing, computer skills, history, sports, environmental studies, languages, building and construction.

THE BEST PART OF MY WEEK:

QUESTIONS I WOULD LIKE TO EXPLORE FURTHER:

MY GOALS FOR NEXT WEEK:

Date: _____

READING

Use this log to record what you read and the amount of time you spend reading each

Monday	*Tuesday*	*Wednesday*	*Thursday*	*Friday*	*Weekend*

EDUCATIONAL EXPERIENCES

Use the spaces below to record the educational experiences you complete this week.

ENGLISH EXPERIENCES:

MATHEMATICS EXPERIENCES:

SCIENCE EXPERIENCES:

EDUCATIONAL OUTINGS

Quote of the Week

'The content of a book holds the power of education and it is with this power that we can shape our future and change lives.'

— Malala Yousafzai

OTHER EDUCATIONAL EXPERIENCES

Use this space to record educational experiences you complete this week in other learning areas

e.g. art, music, wellness and wellbeing, computer skills, history, sports, environmental studies, languages, building and construction.

THE BEST PART OF MY WEEK:

QUESTIONS I WOULD LIKE TO EXPLORE FURTHER:

MY GOALS FOR NEXT WEEK:

Date: _____

READING

Use this log to record what you read and the amount of time you spend reading each

Monday	*Tuesday*	*Wednesday*	*Thursday*	*Friday*	*Weekend*

EDUCATIONAL EXPERIENCES

Use the spaces below to record the educational experiences you complete this week.

ENGLISH EXPERIENCES:

MATHEMATICS EXPERIENCES:

SCIENCE EXPERIENCES:

EDUCATIONAL OUTINGS

Quote of the Week

'Everyone shines, given the right lighting.'

— Susan Cain

OTHER EDUCATIONAL EXPERIENCES

Use this space to record educational experiences you complete this week in other learning areas

e.g. art, music, wellness and wellbeing, computer skills, history, sports, environmental studies, languages, building and construction.

THE BEST PART OF MY WEEK:

QUESTIONS I WOULD LIKE TO EXPLORE FURTHER:

MY GOALS FOR NEXT WEEK:

Date: _____

READING

Use this log to record what you read and the amount of time you spend reading each

| *Monday* | *Tuesday* | *Wednesday* | *Thursday* | *Friday* | *Weekend* |

EDUCATIONAL EXPERIENCES

Use the spaces below to record the educational experiences you complete this week.

ENGLISH EXPERIENCES:

MATHEMATICS EXPERIENCES:

SCIENCE EXPERIENCES:

EDUCATIONAL OUTINGS

Quote of the Week

'An investment in knowledge pays the best interest.'

— Benjamin Franklin

OTHER EDUCATIONAL EXPERIENCES

Use this space to record educational experiences you complete this week in other learning areas

e.g. art, music, wellness and wellbeing, computer skills, history, sports, environmental studies, languages, building and construction.

THE BEST PART OF MY WEEK:

QUESTIONS I WOULD LIKE TO EXPLORE FURTHER:

MY GOALS FOR NEXT WEEK:

Date: _____

READING

Use this log to record what you read and the amount of time you spend reading each

Monday *Tuesday* *Wednesday* *Thursday* *Friday* *Weekend*

EDUCATIONAL EXPERIENCES

Use the spaces below to record the educational experiences you complete this week.

ENGLISH EXPERIENCES:

MATHEMATICS EXPERIENCES:

SCIENCE EXPERIENCES:

EDUCATIONAL OUTINGS

Quote of the Week

'Today you are you! That is truer than true! There is no one alive who is you-er than you!'
— Theodor Seuss Geisel

OTHER EDUCATIONAL EXPERIENCES

Use this space to record educational experiences you complete this week in other learning areas

e.g. art, music, wellness and wellbeing, computer skills, history, sports, environmental studies, languages, building and construction.

THE BEST PART OF MY WEEK:

QUESTIONS I WOULD LIKE TO EXPLORE FURTHER:

MY GOALS FOR NEXT WEEK:

Date: _____

READING

Use this log to record what you read and the amount of time you spend reading each

Monday	*Tuesday*	*Wednesday*	*Thursday*	*Friday*	*Weekend*

EDUCATIONAL EXPERIENCES

Use the spaces below to record the educational experiences you complete this week.

ENGLISH EXPERIENCES:

MATHEMATICS EXPERIENCES:

SCIENCE EXPERIENCES:

EDUCATIONAL OUTINGS

Quote of the Week

'What you do makes a difference, and you have to decide what kind of difference you want to make.'

— Jane Goodall

OTHER EDUCATIONAL EXPERIENCES

Use this space to record educational experiences you complete this week in other learning areas

e.g. art, music, wellness and wellbeing, computer skills, history, sports, environmental studies, languages, building and construction.

THE BEST PART OF MY WEEK:

QUESTIONS I WOULD LIKE TO EXPLORE FURTHER:

MY GOALS FOR NEXT WEEK:

Date: _____

READING

Use this log to record what you read and the amount of time you spend reading each

Monday	Tuesday	Wednesday	Thursday	Friday	Weekend

EDUCATIONAL EXPERIENCES

Use the spaces below to record the educational experiences you complete this week.

ENGLISH EXPERIENCES:

MATHEMATICS EXPERIENCES:

SCIENCE EXPERIENCES:

EDUCATIONAL OUTINGS

Quote of the Week

'Believe you can and you're halfway there.'
— Theodore Roosevelt

OTHER EDUCATIONAL EXPERIENCES

Use this space to record educational experiences you complete this week in other learning areas

e.g. art, music, wellness and wellbeing, computer skills, history, sports, environmental studies, languages, building and construction.

THE BEST PART OF MY WEEK:

QUESTIONS I WOULD LIKE TO EXPLORE FURTHER:

MY GOALS FOR NEXT WEEK:

Date: _____

READING

Use this log to record what you read and the amount of time you spend reading each

Monday	Tuesday	Wednesday	Thursday	Friday	Weekend

EDUCATIONAL EXPERIENCES

Use the spaces below to record the educational experiences you complete this week.

ENGLISH EXPERIENCES:

MATHEMATICS EXPERIENCES:

SCIENCE EXPERIENCES:

EDUCATIONAL OUTINGS

Quote of the Week

'Knowledge isn't power until it is applied.'

— Dale Carnegie

OTHER EDUCATIONAL EXPERIENCES

Use this space to record educational experiences you complete this week in other learning areas

e.g. art, music, wellness and wellbeing, computer skills, history, sports, environmental studies, languages, building and construction.

THE BEST PART OF MY WEEK:

QUESTIONS I WOULD LIKE TO EXPLORE FURTHER:

MY GOALS FOR NEXT WEEK:

Date: _____

READING

Use this log to record what you read and the amount of time you spend reading each

| Monday | Tuesday | Wednesday | Thursday | Friday | Weekend |

EDUCATIONAL EXPERIENCES

Use the spaces below to record the educational experiences you complete this week.

ENGLISH EXPERIENCES:

MATHEMATICS EXPERIENCES:

SCIENCE EXPERIENCES:

EDUCATIONAL OUTINGS

Quote of the Week

'You must never be fearful about what you are doing when it is right.'

— Rosa Parks

OTHER EDUCATIONAL EXPERIENCES

Use this space to record educational experiences you complete this week in other learning areas

e.g. art, music, wellness and wellbeing, computer skills, history, sports, environmental studies, languages, building and construction.

THE BEST PART OF MY WEEK:

QUESTIONS I WOULD LIKE TO EXPLORE FURTHER:

MY GOALS FOR NEXT WEEK:

Date: _____

READING

Use this log to record what you read and the amount of time you spend reading each

Monday	Tuesday	Wednesday	Thursday	Friday	Weekend

EDUCATIONAL EXPERIENCES

Use the spaces below to record the educational experiences you complete this week.

ENGLISH EXPERIENCES:

MATHEMATICS EXPERIENCES:

SCIENCE EXPERIENCES:

EDUCATIONAL OUTINGS

Quote of the Week

'You have brains in your head. You have feet in your shoes. You can steer yourself any direction you choose.'

— *Theodor Seuss Geisel*

OTHER EDUCATIONAL EXPERIENCES

Use this space to record educational experiences you complete this week in other learning areas

e.g. art, music, wellness and wellbeing, computer skills, history, sports, environmental studies, languages, building and construction.

THE BEST PART OF MY WEEK:

QUESTIONS I WOULD LIKE TO EXPLORE FURTHER:

MY GOALS FOR NEXT WEEK:

Date: _____

READING

Use this log to record what you read and the amount of time you spend reading each

Monday	*Tuesday*	*Wednesday*	*Thursday*	*Friday*	*Weekend*

EDUCATIONAL EXPERIENCES

Use the spaces below to record the educational experiences you complete this week.

ENGLISH EXPERIENCES:

MATHEMATICS EXPERIENCES:

SCIENCE EXPERIENCES:

EDUCATIONAL OUTINGS

Quote of the Week

'The most effective way to do it, is to do it.'

— Amelia Earhart

OTHER EDUCATIONAL EXPERIENCES

Use this space to record educational experiences you complete this week in other learning areas

e.g. art, music, wellness and wellbeing, computer skills, history, sports, environmental studies, languages, building and construction.

THE BEST PART OF MY WEEK:

QUESTIONS I WOULD LIKE TO EXPLORE FURTHER:

MY GOALS FOR NEXT WEEK:

Date: _____

READING

Use this log to record what you read and the amount of time you spend reading each

Monday	*Tuesday*	*Wednesday*	*Thursday*	*Friday*	*Weekend*

EDUCATIONAL EXPERIENCES

Use the spaces below to record the educational experiences you complete this week.

ENGLISH EXPERIENCES:

MATHEMATICS EXPERIENCES:

SCIENCE EXPERIENCES:

EDUCATIONAL OUTINGS

Quote of the Week

'Doing the best at this moment puts you in the best place for the next moment.'
— Oprah Winfrey

OTHER EDUCATIONAL EXPERIENCES

Use this space to record educational experiences you complete this week in other learning areas

e.g. art, music, wellness and wellbeing, computer skills, history, sports, environmental studies, languages, building and construction.

THE BEST PART OF MY WEEK:

QUESTIONS I WOULD LIKE TO EXPLORE FURTHER:

MY GOALS FOR NEXT WEEK:

Date: _____

READING

Use this log to record what you read and the amount of time you spend reading each

Monday	*Tuesday*	*Wednesday*	*Thursday*	*Friday*	*Weekend*

EDUCATIONAL EXPERIENCES

Use the spaces below to record the educational experiences you complete this week.

ENGLISH EXPERIENCES:

MATHEMATICS EXPERIENCES:

SCIENCE EXPERIENCES:

EDUCATIONAL OUTINGS

Quote of the Week

'The important thing is to not stop questioning. Curiosity has its own reason for existing.'
— Albert Einstein

OTHER EDUCATIONAL EXPERIENCES

Use this space to record educational experiences you complete this week in other learning areas

e.g. art, music, wellness and wellbeing, computer skills, history, sports, environmental studies, languages, building and construction.

THE BEST PART OF MY WEEK:

QUESTIONS I WOULD LIKE TO EXPLORE FURTHER:

MY GOALS FOR NEXT WEEK:

Date: _____

READING

Use this log to record what you read and the amount of time you spend reading each

Monday	*Tuesday*	*Wednesday*	*Thursday*	*Friday*	*Weekend*

EDUCATIONAL EXPERIENCES

Use the spaces below to record the educational experiences you complete this week.

ENGLISH EXPERIENCES:

MATHEMATICS EXPERIENCES:

SCIENCE EXPERIENCES:

EDUCATIONAL OUTINGS

Quote of the Week

'Success is the ability to go from one failure to another with no loss of enthusiasm.'

— Winston Churchill

OTHER EDUCATIONAL EXPERIENCES

Use this space to record educational experiences you complete this week in other learning areas

e.g. art, music, wellness and wellbeing, computer skills, history, sports, environmental studies, languages, building and construction.

THE BEST PART OF MY WEEK:

QUESTIONS I WOULD LIKE TO EXPLORE FURTHER:

MY GOALS FOR NEXT WEEK:

Date: _____

READING

Use this log to record what you read and the amount of time you spend reading each

| *Monday* | *Tuesday* | *Wednesday* | *Thursday* | *Friday* | *Weekend* |

EDUCATIONAL EXPERIENCES

Use the spaces below to record the educational experiences you complete this week.

ENGLISH EXPERIENCES:

MATHEMATICS EXPERIENCES:

SCIENCE EXPERIENCES:

EDUCATIONAL OUTINGS

Quote of the Week

'When you take risks you learn that there will be times when you succeed and there will be times when you fail and both are equally important.'

— *Ellen DeGeneres*

OTHER EDUCATIONAL EXPERIENCES

Use this space to record educational experiences you complete this week in other learning areas

e.g. art, music, wellness and wellbeing, computer skills, history, sports, environmental studies, languages, building and construction.

THE BEST PART OF MY WEEK:

QUESTIONS I WOULD LIKE TO EXPLORE FURTHER:

MY GOALS FOR NEXT WEEK:

Date: _____

READING

Use this log to record what you read and the amount of time you spend reading each

Monday	Tuesday	Wednesday	Thursday	Friday	Weekend

EDUCATIONAL EXPERIENCES

Use the spaces below to record the educational experiences you complete this week.

ENGLISH EXPERIENCES:

MATHEMATICS EXPERIENCES:

SCIENCE EXPERIENCES:

EDUCATIONAL OUTINGS

Quote of the Week

'If you're walking down the right path and you're willing to keep walking, eventually you'll make progress.'

— Barack Obama

OTHER EDUCATIONAL EXPERIENCES

Use this space to record educational experiences you complete this week in other learning areas

e.g. art, music, wellness and wellbeing, computer skills, history, sports, environmental studies, languages, building and construction.

THE BEST PART OF MY WEEK:

QUESTIONS I WOULD LIKE TO EXPLORE FURTHER:

MY GOALS FOR NEXT WEEK:

Date: _____

READING

Use this log to record what you read and the amount of time you spend reading each

Monday	Tuesday	Wednesday	Thursday	Friday	Weekend

EDUCATIONAL EXPERIENCES

Use the spaces below to record the educational experiences you complete this week.

ENGLISH EXPERIENCES:

MATHEMATICS EXPERIENCES:

SCIENCE EXPERIENCES:

EDUCATIONAL OUTINGS

Quote of the Week

*'Start where you are.
Use what you have.
Do what you can.'*

— Arthur Ashe

OTHER EDUCATIONAL EXPERIENCES

Use this space to record educational experiences you complete this week in other learning areas

e.g. art, music, wellness and wellbeing, computer skills, history, sports, environmental studies, languages, building and construction.

THE BEST PART OF MY WEEK:

QUESTIONS I WOULD LIKE TO EXPLORE FURTHER:

MY GOALS FOR NEXT WEEK:

Date: _____

READING

Use this log to record what you read and the amount of time you spend reading each

Monday	*Tuesday*	*Wednesday*	*Thursday*	*Friday*	*Weekend*

EDUCATIONAL EXPERIENCES

Use the spaces below to record the educational experiences you complete this week.

ENGLISH EXPERIENCES:

MATHEMATICS EXPERIENCES:

SCIENCE EXPERIENCES:

EDUCATIONAL OUTINGS

Quote of the Week

'I believe that education is all about being excited about something. Seeing passion and enthusiasm helps push an educational message.'

— Steve Irwin

OTHER EDUCATIONAL EXPERIENCES

Use this space to record educational experiences you complete this week in other learning areas

e.g. art, music, wellness and wellbeing, computer skills, history, sports, environmental studies, languages, building and construction.

THE BEST PART OF MY WEEK:

QUESTIONS I WOULD LIKE TO EXPLORE FURTHER:

MY GOALS FOR NEXT WEEK:

Date: _____

READING

Use this log to record what you read and the amount of time you spend reading each

Monday	*Tuesday*	*Wednesday*	*Thursday*	*Friday*	*Weekend*

EDUCATIONAL EXPERIENCES

Use the spaces below to record the educational experiences you complete this week.

ENGLISH EXPERIENCES:

MATHEMATICS EXPERIENCES:

SCIENCE EXPERIENCES:

EDUCATIONAL OUTINGS

Quote of the Week

'By education, I mean an all-round drawing of the best in child and man in body, mind and spirit.'
— Mahatma Ghandi

OTHER EDUCATIONAL EXPERIENCES

Use this space to record educational experiences you complete this week in other learning areas

e.g. art, music, wellness and wellbeing, computer skills, history, sports, environmental studies, languages, building and construction.

THE BEST PART OF MY WEEK:

QUESTIONS I WOULD LIKE TO EXPLORE FURTHER:

MY GOALS FOR NEXT WEEK:

Date: _____

READING

Use this log to record what you read and the amount of time you spend reading each

Monday	Tuesday	Wednesday	Thursday	Friday	Weekend

EDUCATIONAL EXPERIENCES

Use the spaces below to record the educational experiences you complete this week.

ENGLISH EXPERIENCES:

MATHEMATICS EXPERIENCES:

SCIENCE EXPERIENCES:

EDUCATIONAL OUTINGS

Quote of the Week

'Take criticism seriously, but not personally. If there is truth or merit in the criticism, try to learn from it. Otherwise, let it roll right off you.'
— Hilary Clinton

OTHER EDUCATIONAL EXPERIENCES

Use this space to record educational experiences you complete this week in other learning areas

e.g. art, music, wellness and wellbeing, computer skills, history, sports, environmental studies, languages, building and construction.

THE BEST PART OF MY WEEK:

QUESTIONS I WOULD LIKE TO EXPLORE FURTHER:

MY GOALS FOR NEXT WEEK:

Date: _____

READING

Use this log to record what you read and the amount of time you spend reading each

Monday	*Tuesday*	*Wednesday*	*Thursday*	*Friday*	*Weekend*

EDUCATIONAL EXPERIENCES

Use the spaces below to record the educational experiences you complete this week.

ENGLISH EXPERIENCES:

MATHEMATICS EXPERIENCES:

SCIENCE EXPERIENCES:

EDUCATIONAL OUTINGS

Quote of the Week

'Courage is what it takes to stand up and speak, it's also what it takes to sit down and listen.'
— Winston Churchill

OTHER EDUCATIONAL EXPERIENCES

Use this space to record educational experiences you complete this week in other learning areas

e.g. art, music, wellness and wellbeing, computer skills, history, sports, environmental studies, languages, building and construction.

THE BEST PART OF MY WEEK:

QUESTIONS I WOULD LIKE TO EXPLORE FURTHER:

MY GOALS FOR NEXT WEEK:

Holidays

Use the space below to stick in any photographs, keepsakes or tokens.

Holiday Memories

Holidays

Use the space below to stick in any photographs, keepsakes or tokens.

Holiday Memories

Holidays

Use the space below to stick in any photographs, keepsakes or tokens.

Holiday Memories

Holidays

Use the space below to stick in any photographs, keepsakes or tokens.

Holiday Memories

Holidays

Use the space below to stick in any photographs, keepsakes or tokens.

Holiday Memories

Holidays

Use the space below to stick in any photographs, keepsakes or tokens.

Holiday Memories

Learning by Topic Frameworks Explained

Education Boutique's *Learning by Topic Frameworks* are carefully and individually constructed to support learners of all different ages and abilities.

Learning by Topic Frameworks can also be referred to as thematic units, integrated units, connected outcome groups and contracts. It is the process of children learning across all learning areas/subjects through a single topic (in this case a personalised and interest-based topic).

They have been proven to assist and enhance learning for children with a variety of needs and skills:

- Children learning English as an additional language
- Gifted and talented children (the units promote higher order thinking - thinking outside the box)
- Children with autism and other additional needs
- Reluctant learners

Our frameworks encourage children to be investigators, observers, explorers and creators. We encourage children to take ownership of their learning and all educational experiences are written in child friendly and child directed language.

We all work better and learn more effectively when we are engaged and interested in the task at hand and Education Boutique's *Learning by Topic Frameworks* support interest based and child lead learning.

We have a bank of existing frameworks on a variety of topics and also create bespoke frameworks to meet the individual student's interest. For more information on the frameworks please visit: www.educationboutique.co.uk.

ENGLISH

- Theme/Spelling words: agriculture, sustainability, conserve, natural, resources, environment, legumes, nutritious, consumers, dietary.
- List spellings in alphabetical order; write synonyms and antonyms for words (where appropriate); create a crossword puzzle for your theme words; write your theme words in sentences or use all of them in a short story, include effective language e.g. similes, metaphors, alliteration and personification.
- What is sustainable eating and why is it becoming increasingly important? Carry out some research and summarise in two or three paragraphs. (Genre of writing: Discussion)
- What are the benefits of shopping locally, growing your own fruit and veg and eating seasonally?
- Write a letter to people within your local community encouraging them to shop local and eat seasonally. (Genre of writing: Persuasive) *TT: You may also want to record this in the style of a vlog.
- What is the problem with palm oil and what sustainable options are being/have been put in place?
- Write a diary entry from the point of view of an orangutan whose habitat has just been destroyed by deforestation for the purpose of sourcing palm oil. (Genre of writing: Recount/Narrative)
- Imagine you are a tree or plant. What advice would you give to humans about caring for the environment? Write a list of dos and don'ts.
- Write a story about an unlikely friendship between an orangutan and a woodcutter/lumberjack/logger (choose which term you want to use). (Genre of writing: Narrative)
- Write a poem in sonnet format about the current state of our planet and how we can change our ways to ensure sustainability.

SCIENCE

- List different ways we use plants in our lives.
- Design a meal plan that ensures a balanced, varied and sustainable diet. *TT: You could represent one of the meals on a paper plate with 'food' made from recyclable materials. List on your meal plan where the food should be sourced from to ensure sustainability.
- Decide on what you can plant in your own garden to do your part in supporting sustainable eating. Consider seasons when you are planning and planting; plan to be able to source fresh produce from your garden all year round.

LEARNING BY TOPIC FRAMEWORK
SUSTAINABLE EATING

MATHEMATICS

- What are the deforestation figures for the Amazon Rainforest over the past decade? Have they increased or decreased? Plot this data on a line graph.
- Calculate the volume of any planter boxes or garden beds you have access to.
- Create a number code for the alphabet (e.g. a =1 b=2, be a bit more adventurous than this example) write your theme words using this code – can anyone crack your codes?
- Now ask an adult to write some addition, subtraction, multiplication and division sums in this code. Can you decode these?
- Find the perimeter and area of your garden, planter boxes or garden beds.
- Measure different angles around your garden or local environment. Maybe take some photos and then sort them into a table with the heading, acute angles, right angles, obtuse angles, straight angles and reflex angles. *TT: You can either print photos for this activity or construct your table on the computer and cut and paste the photos in.
- From your science activity that involved you planning and planting your own fruit and veg, calculate how much your family might save in their weekly shopping over a year if everything you plan to plant thrives. To work this out you will also have to take into account the costs of the equipment you needed to plant your fruit and veg.
- What 3D shapes can you identify around your garden? Can you list/label the properties for each shape? E.g. number of faces and vertices.
- Once a seedling appears (from your Science activity) measure the height of it every morning and every night until the bud appears. Then plot these measurements on a line graph to show its growth/progress.

ART / DESIGN AND TECHNOLOGY

- Create an exhibition of photographs titled "Sustainable Eating". *TT: If you are going to include photos of public spaces (e.g. a farmers' market) make sure you ask permission of any stall holders you might be photographing.
- Create a piece of artwork from fallen twigs and leaves.
- Come up with an alternative and reusable packaging product for people to use to pack their fruit and veg at the supermarket. In many supermarkets the only option is single use plastic bags.

PSHE / MUSIC

- PSHE: Design a poster or advertising campaign that creates awareness of the benefits of sustainable eating. *TT: You may like to film a TV commercial as part of your advertising campaign. (CC: Art)
- Music: Create a rap or jingle as part of your advertising campaign!
- PSHE: Are there any items/products in your house that contain palm oil? Could any of them be replaced with alternative palm oil free products? *TT: Palm oil can come under many names, look up the different ways it can be listed on products before you begin this activity.

NOTE

Note: You can choose how you would like to carry out and present many of these learning experiences. You may want to create PowerPoint presentations, write some blogs or record vlogs. Some experiences may be more suited to having a discussion with a family member or friend.

LEARNING BY TOPIC FRAMEWORK

THE ENVIRONMENT

KEY

CC: *Cross Curricular*

*TT: *Top Tip*

Suggested Reading/Documentary List:

- *Our Planet:* David Attenborough documentary
- *World Without Fish*, by Mark Kurlansky (10+)
- *Save the Planet: Local Farms and Sustainable Foods*, by Julia Vogel

Suggested Educational Outing:

- Can you find any sustainable food restaurants or markets near where you live?

HISTORY

- Look into the history of Fair Trade and outline key facts.
- Find an image of the Amazon Rainforest from 50 or so years ago and find an image from today showing the effects of deforestation. Compare and contrast these images.
- What has happened to the planet to make sustainable eating such an important issue in current times?
- What are your predictions for the future in regards to sustainable eating?

GEOGRAPHY

- What are the effects of deforestation?
- What could be done in your community to see beneficial changes to your local environment?
- Find out where you can shop for fresh and local produce in your community/borough/county (e.g. farm shops, farmers markets etc)
- On a map, locate and plot areas around the world that have been significantly damaged by deforestation.

My Online Learning Resource Notes

MY HOME ED JOURNAL

$$1+2=3$$

Glossary of Terms—Mathematics

NUMBER

algebra
The study of symbols in mathematics

array
To represent/arrange information in rows – typically where multiplication is concerned, e.g. 3 rows of 4

chronological
In order – referring to time

decimal point
A decimal point is used when representing a whole number and a fraction, e.g. 4.57

denominator
The bottom number/the number under the line in a fraction

difference
Another word for subtraction

equivalent fractions
Fractions of the same value, e.g. 4/16 = 2/8 = 1/4

factor
Numbers that when multiplied together equal a specific number - they are factors of that specific number, e.g. 3 and 4 are factors of 12

fraction
A part of a whole number

improper fraction
The numerator is larger than the denominator, e.g. 9/4

inverse
The opposite of a particular method, e.g. division is the inverse operation to multiplication

mixed fraction
A whole number alongside a proper fraction, e.g. 8 1/2

numerator
The top number/the number above the line in a fraction

ordinal number
Represents the position of something, e.g. first/1st, second/2nd

percentage
A fraction of 100, represented using the following symbol: %

prime number
A whole number that is greater than 1 and its only factors are one and itself

product
Another word for multiplication

proper fractions
The numerator is smaller than the denominator

remainder
An amount that is left over, e.g. 14 ÷ 3 = 4 R 2 (remainder two)

square number
Multiplying a number by itself, e.g. $6^2 = 36$

square root
The opposite/inverse of a square number, e.g. $\sqrt{36} = 6$

MEASUREMENT AND DATA

analogue time
Time represented by an hour hand and a minute hand

anticlockwise
The opposite to the direction hands on a clock move

area
The space inside a 2D shape or surface

capacity
How much something can hold, typically measured in litres and millilitres

clockwise
The direction hands on a clock move

data
Gathering information and often recording/representing it with tally marks and graphs

digital time
Hours and minutes represented with numbers, usually in 24-hour time

estimate
A rough calculation that involves drawing on your knowledge

gradient
The slope of a straight line

linear
Data that can be represented by a straight line on a graph

mass
Measuring the weight of an object

mean
The average of a group of numbers. To find the mean add up the numbers and then divide by how many numbers there are

median
The number in the middle of a group of numbers, place the numbers in order from smallest to largest and the number in the middle is the median. Where there is an even amount of numbers the median is found by adding the two middle numbers together and dividing them by two

mode
The number that appears most frequently in a group of numbers

perimeter
The measurement of the distance around the sides of a 2D shape

probability
Determining how likely something is to happen, this is usually represented as a fraction, decimal or parentage

range
The difference between the largest and smallest number in a group of numbers

ratio
Shows how much of one item compared to another item

GEOMETRY

acute angle
An angle between 0 and 90°

axis
Reference lines on graphs and grids where coordinates are plotted

bisector
A geometrical term meaning to cut into two equal parts

circumference
The distance around a circle

coordinates
A pair of numbers that show a position on a graph or map

degree
How angles are measured

diameter
The length of a line through the centre of a circle

horizontal line
A line that runs across

obtuse angle
An angle between 90° and 180°

parallel lines
Straight lines that are the same distance apart

perpendicular
Two lines that are at right angles to one another

radius
The measured distance from the centre of a circle to its edge (half the diameter)

reflex angle
An angle between 180° and 360°

right angle
A 90° angle

straight angle
A 180° angle

vertex
Another word for the corner of a shape

vertical line
A line that runs up and down

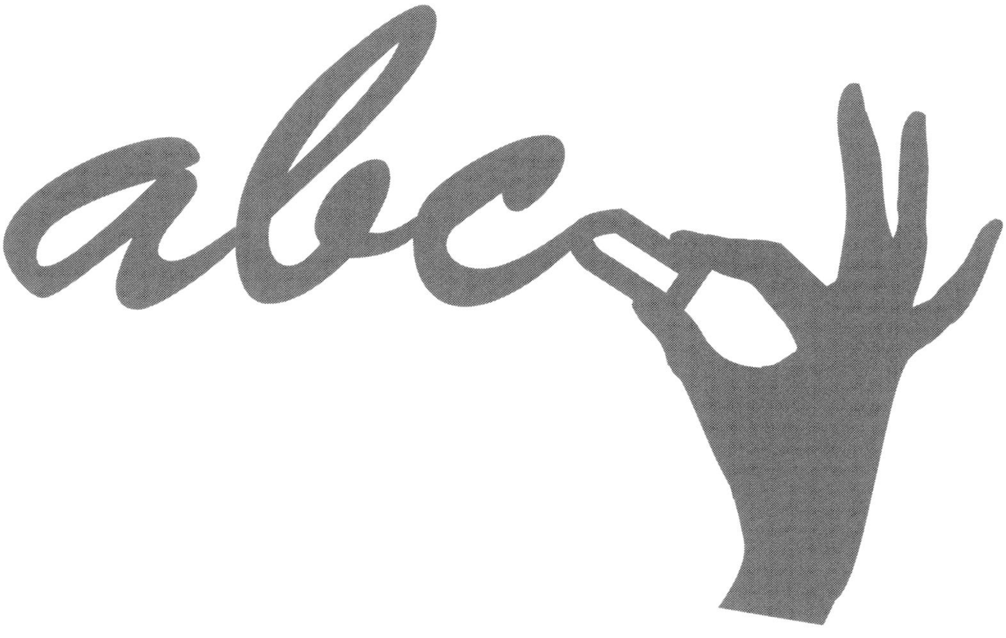
abc

Glossary of Terms–English

WORD TYPES, SENTENCES AND GRAMMAR

adjectival phrase
A phrase starting with an adjective that describes a noun

adjective
A describing word

adverb
A word that describes an adjective or a verb

adverbial clause
A group of words that carry out the same purpose as an adverb

antonym
A word that has an opposite meaning to another word

clause
A group of words that include a subject and a verb

colloquialism
Informal and casual words and phrases

complex sentence
A sentence that has a subordinate clause/s

compound sentence
A sentence with a minimum of two independent clauses, usually joined by a conjunction/connective

compound words
When existing words are put together to form a new word, e.g. tooth and brush = toothbrush

conjunction/connective
Words that connect clauses and phrases, e.g. and, but, because

consonant
A letter/sound – excluding vowels

contraction
Combining and shortening two words using an apostrophe, e.g. did not – didn't

determiner
Words that identify and precede a noun,
e.g. the, a, an, that

dialogue
Conversations in written form, usually represented using speech/quotation marks (unless in script form)

exclamation
A statement that expresses excitement/emotion

homophone
Words that are pronounced the same but have different meanings and spellings

hyperbole
Exaggerations - they are not meant to be taken literally

interjection
Parts of speech used to communicate emotion, e.g. phew, oops, shh

phrase
A group of words that does not include a subject or verb

noun
A person, place or thing

object
In a sentence, the object is the thing or person an action is being focussed towards

pronoun
Words used in place of a noun to avoid repetition, e.g. he, she, they, it

predicate
A part of a sentence or clause that contains a verb and explains the action

ple sentence
A sentence made up of one independent clause, containing one subject and a predicate

statement
A common type of sentence that most typically ends with a full stop

subject
In a sentence the subject is the person, place or thing that carries out the action/verb

subordinate clause
A clause containing a subject and verb, it does not make sense on its own

synonym
A word that has the same or a similar meaning to another word

verb
An action (doing) word

tense
Writing in the past or present

vowel
The following five letters: a, e, i, o, u

PUNCTUATION AND WORD STRUCTURE

apostrophe '
Used for contractions or to show possession

brackets ( )
Used to add extra information and detail to a sentence

bullet point •
Used for lists and to break down and highlight key information

colon :
Used to introduce a list or to separate clauses

comma ,
Used to list items in a sentence, used after/between phrases and clauses and used to replace words to avoid repetition

dash -
Can be used in a similar way to brackets and used to represent an interruption in dialogue

ellipsis …
Can be used for dramatic effect/suspense and the trailing off of a thought

exclamation mark !
Used at the end of an exclamation - a statement that expresses excitement/emotion

full stop .
Used at the end of a statement – a common sentence

inverted commas " " or ' '
Used to highlight speech/dialogue and quotes in writing

paragraph
Used to break up and structure writing. You start a new paragraph when there is a change in person, place or time

prefix
Letters placed at the beginning of a root word that will change the meaning

root word
A word in its simplest form – without a prefix or suffix

semicolon ;
Used to separate two, closely related, main clauses. A semicolon can replace a connective

suffix
Letters placed at the end of a root word that will change or enhance the meaning

question mark ?
Used at the end of a question

TYPES OF WRITING

descriptive text
The description of a person, place or thing using quality adjectives, adverbs and action words, along with vivid sensory details and figurative language.

fiction
Make believe and imaginative writing

first person
Writing as yourself (or as a group) and about yourself

instructional text
A set of instructions that detail how to make or do something e.g. cook a recipe, assemble a toy or piece of furniture

narrative text
Story writing which will contain a main character, a plot and have a clear beginning, middle and end

non-fiction
Factual writing about real events, people, animals and places

persuasive text
Writing that aims to convince the reader to take the same side of the argument as the writer

poetry
Descriptive, imaginative and/or emotional writing with a certain rhythm and style

recount
Writing about an event/events that have already taken place

second person
Writing where you address someone else (usually the reader) with words such as you and your

third person
When you write/tell the story about other people. You are taking on the role of the narrator

EFFECTIVE LANGUAGE FEATURES

alliteration
When words with the same sound and/or letter are used alongside one another in a sentence or phrase

idiom
A phrase or sentence that's meaning is not meant to be taken literally

metaphor
A direct comparison that is not meant to be taken literally

onomatopoeia
Words that are written to imitate sound, e.g. roar, buzz, rattle

personification
To give something that isn't human (an animal or an object), human characteristics

simile
Using the words as or like to compare things

rhetorical question
A question used for effect that doesn't have or necessitate an answer

Printed in Great Britain
by Amazon